Th

THE KNOT

Ruth Fainlight

HUTCHINSON
London Sydney Auckland Johannesburg

© Ruth Fainlight 1990

This edition first published in 1990 by
Hutchinson

Century Hutchinson Ltd, 20 Vauxhall Bridge Road,
London SW1V 2SA

Century Hutchinson Australia, 20 Alfred Street,
Milsons Point, Sydney NSW 2061, Australia.

Century Hutchinson New Zealand Limited
PO Box 40–086, Glenfield, Auckland 10, New Zealand

Century Hutchinson South Africa (Pty) Ltd
PO Box 337, Bergvlei, 2012 South Africa

Set in Times by Input Typesetting Ltd, London
Printed and bound in Great Britain by
Cox and Wyman, Reading.

British Library Cataloguing in Publication Data
Fainlight, Ruth
  The knot.
  I. Title
  811.54

  ISBN 0–09–174294–3

Acknowledgements

Agenda, Critical Quarterly, Encounter, English, Hudson Review, Jewish Chronicle, Lettre Internationale, Lines Review, Literary Review, London Magazine, London Review of Books, The New Yorker, The Orange Dove of Fiji: Poems for the World Wide Fund for Nature, Outposts, The Oxford Magazine, The Pen, PEN Anthology: New Poetry II, Poetry Book Society Anthology, 1988–89, *Poetry Durham, Poetry Review, Prospice, The Reaper, Threepenny Review, Times Literary Supplement, Vanderbilt Review, Two plus Two, Word and Image, Yale Review.*

Between the Canyons, A Discussion with Patrick Kavanagh and *The Same Power* were first published in Mir Poets pamphlet number 7.

Contents

The Knot

The Knot

One of them showed me how to split a reed
and plait it into a holder for my hammock.
'When you know you've got to get away,' she said,
'use this piece of cloth, faded red, and knot
it tight at either end. Find somewhere far
from the children and dogs and vague old people,
the women thumping grain, those noisy men
around the smoky fire. Loop it under a branch
or over a beam in one of the empty huts
at the edge of the clearing. Then crawl inside,
when you need to be alone to hear the story,
the story you tell yourself all day but sometimes
cannot hear.' And sometimes, there in my hammock,
words would come and cluster together like wasps
between the poles and matting of the roof
as black as rotting fruit or drying membrane,
a blossom of words in a dusty ray of light.
Words would form a knot and start a story.

The European Story

1

A story? There's not enough action –
just an endless loping
through the cobwebbed aisles and arches
of a Gothic forest unreeling
like a painted backcloth. Then he stumbles,
and the heart in the cup of his bloodied palm
bounces into the ferns.

Red-cheeked, rawboned, black moustachioed,
a puppet escaped from its master, a soldier
on the run, he served the story's purpose –
did the murder, cut her open.
Now he doesn't matter.
The heart becomes the drama's centre.
Its voice calls out: 'My son, my son,
have you hurt yourself? My dear, don't fall!'

2

My mother might have told that story.
Cave-crone guarding the fire-spark
as safe inside its ball of clay and moss
as an infant lapped by womb-water,
she handed on the ancient curse
(the lesson I refused to learn)
mother-tongue mumbling heart-words.

Last breath from an open mouth,
moisture beads the fluttering threads
spiders wove between the branches
and makes a nimbus of splintered light
through tear-clogged lashes, a pearl-encrusted

iconostasis of wonderworkers
to prove Death weaker than mother-love,
and reconcile the sacrificial daughters.

3

I was born in a smothering caul,
a veiled woman. My first cry was a protest.
I feared the antlered maskers' shadows,
the rooting goddess who eats her farrow,
the touch of Balder's frost-burned mistletoe.
In dreams I was the puppet-killer,
her defender, with sword and dagger sharper
than the Angel's, armour brighter than Joan's.

I have danced as either partner
been tormented and tormenter
but could not find the right disguise
to fool her – neither child nor mother
with my child. Oh what grief, never
to hear that special note in her voice:
'My son, my son, have you hurt yourself?'
You want to plunge the knife in your own heart.

4

Cast your bread on the waters.
But the Old Man of the Sea
rises up and straddles your shoulders,
tightens his grip on your windpipe.
There's salt in your mouth.
He's wet and cold and heavy.
You stagger and almost drown.

Then up from the ground between your feet
another one comes
and splits you open,

thrusts his hand in the shambles,
wrenches out your heart.
When he stumbles and drops it, the heart
cries out, My dear, don't fall!

5
A fish appears with a ring in its mouth
and three questions. An old woman
asks for shelter. If you pass the test
each wish is granted until the last

unless it is
to break the mould,
open out a parchment scroll,
cherubim and gargoyles
twining down the margins,
throstles perched on gilded letters,
leafy plants and scaly dragons,
and let the variations flourish,
to change the definitions
of feminine and masculine,
son and mother, love and duty,
and that final one, 'The End':
tell the story different every time.

6
Change the heart into a ticking bomb,
the soldier to a girl – a terrorist,
the very last Crusader,
sure that a dark annunciation chose her
to save the Holy Places of the planet
by casual explosion.
That moves the story on.

Her ideas and actions must be examined
as carefully as a bomb's fuse and circuit,
with the tender skill a surgeon uses
cutting live flesh to open up a heart.
She has been formed by what the story means.
It started in Europe. It spread like radiation.
There's no immunity to images.

On the Theme of Artifice

'Himself, may be, the irreducible X
at the bottom of imagined artifice.'

What does Wallace Stevens mean? I've pondered
those lines, trying to decide if the imagined

must always be artificial – mind's
construction upon, and against, Nature, which he

projects into a pineapple that looms
gigantic as the jar in Tennessee.

       *   *   *

It seems a form of magic: the poet artful
enough to draw the essence of reality

like a shawl, cobweb fine, through a golden ring,
or from the mouth of a bottle coax out the genie

who surges to a mushroom cloud. The same
thought that split the atom, had to imagine

its irreducible nucleus
and the artifice of Time and Space, first.

       *   *   *

At the bottom of imagined artifice,
rather than familiar gods and demons

and current versions of total destruction, he
himself is dreaming pineapples and jars.

The Yellow Plate

i.m. A. G.

A painted plate, yellow-glazed below
the shallow curve of its white porcelain rim,
(yellow I'm always drawn to:
the saffron robe of a mendicant
    or the silk curtains a friend bought in Burma,
    mine now, because she's dead),
is the yellow road of the sun –
that bright furrow plowed between the stars.

Underneath is the painter's complex square mark,
lacquer red, and round scarlet stickers reading:
'Chia ching' and '1796 to
1820'. On the front, twelve creatures.

It took a long time to see
they were the Chinese zodiac,
animal, bird, and reptile, real
or imagined (the one in the centre
is a dragon, not a crocodile),
that give names to the hours of the day
and the little twelve-day cycle,
the months of the year and the sixty years
I guess was the expected life span
of those hunters and shepherds.
    When she died, my friend was younger.

Tradition has it that Tajao, a minister
of Emperor Hwang-ti, circa
2697 BC, invented them.
So little has changed since, the same

17

names are still used, (though I can't compute
what our year is by that calendar,
nor my own sign), and I sensed before
I knew what they meant and were.

The colours are green and red and yellow –
jade, cinnabar, and sulphur,
the drawn line blackish sepia.
A pale wash of pink fills
the bodies of the wrinkle-snouted pig
and the rat, whose ideograph is 'water'.
Too anxious for the luxury
of variation, the rabbit is pure white.

Cloudy patterns blotch the horse,
whose mane and tail fall fine and soft
as new-washed hair, and the bristling dog,
like shadow dappling windblown corn.
Flamey stripes unite the horned sheep and
the thoughtful tiger biting a raised paw.
Dragon and serpent are scaled, checkered
and barred, their dangerous twirling tongues
high-voltage warnings.

The hen looks fierce as a cock, crested
and hook-clawed, not domestic
and submissive like the ox
with a rope through its round nostril.
The monkey has delicate hands, subtle
lips, and watchful eyes – a courtier
wondering if he's telling the right story.

Everything about the plate – all
the moods and colours, characters and patterns –
    she was like all of it,
    as beautiful.

Flower Feet

(silk shoes in the Whitworth Museum, Manchester)

Real women's feet wore these objects
that look like toys or spectacle cases stitched
from bands of coral, jade, and apricot silk
embroidered with twined sprays of flowers.
Those hearts, tongues, crescents and discs, leather
shapes an inch across, are the soles of shoes
no wider or longer than the span of my ankle.

If the feet had been cut off and the raw stumps
thrust inside the openings, surely
it could not hurt more than broken toes, twisted
back and bandaged tight. An old woman,
leaning on a cane outside her door
in a Chinese village, smiled to tell how
she fought and cried, how when she stood on points
of pain that gnawed like fire, nurse and mother
praised her tottering walk on flower feet.
Her friends nodded, glad the times had changed.
Otherwise, they would have crippled their daughters.

Poppies

A bed of them
looks like a dressing room
backstage after the chorus changed costume,

ruffled heaps
of papery orange petticoats
and slick pink satin bodices.

Every petal's base
is marked with the same
confident black smear as a painted eyelid

and the frill
of jostling purple anthers
sifts a powdery kohl that clogs the lashes

shading watchful glances
from dilating pupils, as though
all the dancers swallowed belladonna.

The pleated velvet star
at the centre of each flower
is the top of a box filled with jet beads.

The hard green buds
are their husbands' fists, the silver-
bristled leaves are their admirers' beards.

The Worm

A schoolgirl in a bus queue on Sloane Street
was staring intently, her sweet young face
distorted by repulsion and pity,
at an earthworm. Its central part was pale
and crushed down flat, the ends engorged and dark
and still writhing. That particular pink,
like raw membrane tinged with oily orange
shading into purple, or a nameless
scrap of butcher's trimmings (nothing could look
more naked), glistened on the wet pavement.

The one who'd done it must have hurried on,
too distracted to notice where she trod.
Between the line of people and the row
of pointed iron railings enclosing
sooty greenery, the worm awaited
the next decisive footfall. I wanted
to pick it up, put it out of harm's way
on some soil or a leaf to heal or die.
I have enjoyed the touch of loam and marl
and mud on my hands, breaking cold clay clods
to find the live red seam of worm inside.

Then I imagined that action seen through
the schoolgirl's eyes, and those other people's.
I hesitated and lost conviction,
doubting my impulse – which made me feel
a pious fraud, not even squeamish enough.

Flies

November sun as warm as a Levantine
winter made me push my window up
this morning, brought back donkey-drivers' calls,
the look and smell of bakers' stalls and offal
butchers. (Flies were everywhere.)

But the shudder of glass (fear a splintering shard
might pierce me) from the frame I carelessly jammed askew,
as heavy lorries brake and lower gear
to take the corner for a shortcut to the A40,
changed those images to Home County:
a pan of clarifying sugar syrup
on the Aga wrinkling as it starts to boil
(the crab-apple jelly-bag dripping draws flies
to the kitchen) or the irritable twitch
of a horse's flank to shift the biting flies.

The noise I heard could have been
the drone of a distant combine harvester,
a helicopter spraying, or closer still
here in town, a treadle-machine next door
(that new family must be tailors) with their
muffled hullabaloo through the party wall (they're
killing each other: the flies are driving them crazy).

So I went to put the window down, to stop
the thrumming and its associations, and found
summer's last fly, trapped by the double-glazing.

Early Rivers

This jar of rosy-purple jam is labelled
'Early Rivers, August 82' –
the date I made it, the name the farmer gave
those plums, smooth as onyx eggs, but warmer.

The dimpled groove, bloom-dusted, down each fruit
pouted at the touch of my knife, yielding
the stone I put inside a cotton sock
(relict of a worn-out pair – every
boiling dyed it darker crimson – from one
plum-season to the next I saved it) then pushed
the lumpy tied-up bag into the centre of
the pulpy amber halves and melting sugar
in the preserving kettle, and let the mixture
ooze its pectins, odours, juices, flavours,

until the chemistry of time and fire
produced this sharpness, sweetness, that I'm eating
now, straight from the jar, smearing my mouth,
digging the spoon in deeper, seeking a taste
undiluted even by nostalgia.

August

August is like a woman who's already thinking
that she'll soon be forty. There's something old-fashioned
about her, emanating a womanly odour
of sachets. You can tell that she's been badly treated
by men. Her daughter has left home. She's probably
divorced. She's the manageress of a dress shop.

One might talk of her carriage: she seems to be wearing
a corset. She's quite large and very white skinned.
Her hair is set, her face is powdered matt, and her
thin and rather mournful little mouth with lips
firmly closed on each other except when she bites
them, is carefully painted and always looks wet.

August is the month when everything stops growing.
She feels she stopped growing a long time ago; though
she wouldn't put it like that. She doesn't believe in
too much introspection. Dignified and solitary,
she walks through the park after work, under
the heavy, dusty, dying green of August trees.

The Neville Brothers

(at Vanderbilt University, Nashville, Tennessee, Spring 1985)

As soon as he walked on stage, I saw
that the lead singer was Lord Krishna
wearing a sleeveless red T-shirt, jeans
and high heels. He was gorgeous. In the dim
blue exit lights of the auditorium,
adoring him, we were all milkmaids.

I'd bought pictures of faces like his, full cheeked,
almond eyed, from Bombay street vendors.
Just this side of fat, those shoulders
and pectorals for the moment are perfect.
A lush male torso slowly swayed
as nervous legs pranced and pawed like a horse.

Amplified drumbeats were driving them wild.
How often before he had watched tranced
devotees or dawn dancers wanting
more and louder, like the audience now.
But this was a concert on campus, not
the Juggernaut temple, or a bar in New Orleans.

Rock Island

for Jane and Vereen Bell

Deep pools in the stone bed of the river.
A dry pavement between tumbled rocks
and boulders. Jade yellow of flowing water.
The wide valley closed by limestone bluffs.
Soft tones of blue sky and small white clouds.
Bright greenness of new leaves and buds.

The pale fungus, the litter of bark and branches
from fallen, broken trees along the hill.
Confusion of greyness against earth's redness.
I pulled a mushroom, tall and bullet-like
with a gun-metal glint, and turned it over.
The gills looked inky, sooty, dangerous.

Possum or raccoon, the dark-furred creature
that ignored my nearness? It emanated
misery, a concentration of pain
and stillness I could not understand until
I watched those dead back legs slowly dragged
across the field's rough grass into a ditch.

In Tuscaloosa –

    a puppy trotted down from a verandah
past the yard-sprinkler, and led me to
the corner of an avenue
where oaks were swagged with mauve wisteria.

Breathless and excited as an orphan
I watched a misty nimbus form
around the streetlamps and glowing from
windows of houses where I knew no one.

Out on the Porch

Who expects the whole bus queue
she passes while shopping,
like a chorus of gossiping aunts and neighbours
or the row of sunflowers, obediently heliotropic,
shading the porch where they sit and watch her,
to forget everything else, wishing her luck?

Whose neck stiffens and spine arches
trying to do what they want (she can't be
that much younger, yet still feels débutante),
desperate for approval.
It makes her eyes itch with exasperation –
like saying a poem for the aunts and neighbours

then later, from an upstairs window, hearing
that tolerant laughter out on the porch
over clinking teacups and impatient slaps
at mosquitoes as they change the subject.
Who insisted? Who arranged it?
Thank God when the bus comes.

Rachel

Do you remember the Indian burn?
Lucy backed me against the wall,
Dolores closed her hand on my arm,
and as though she were wringing out a towel
twisted in opposite directions.

They laughed the laugh of the bigger and older
but not so clever, then let me go,
to trawl the playground for more fun.
The mark glowed like a brand on my skin
but revenge was only for Superman.

Rachel was the new girl. She didn't wear
sloppy joes and saddle shoes
but an odd dress, and her hair fell
in loose curls. She looked like a gipsy,
or like myself. It made me nervous.

She could hum the rest of the tune
when the record stopped in Music
Appreciation, recite the names
of other books by Dickens:
the friend of my imaginings.

Yet until then, I'd been the one
who might have drawn Miss Taylor's smile
across the unresponsive classroom. Now,
something seemed to weight my arm
and block my tongue, just as it did

when Dolores and Lucy dragged Rachel
into the corner behind the toilets and,
glad to avoid their attentions, I laughed
with the others while she struggled and wept.
Her glance hurt more than an Indian burn.

Off the Interstate

Following instructions
we stopped at every viewpoint
around the Painted Desert.
Mineral deposits
streaked like bird-droppings
over faded purples,
bled-out pinks and reds.
It looked like a crater filled
with cooling clinker under
rainclouds that might have been
smoke from its last eruption.

At the Petrified Forest
an elderly man in the car park
started to talk about Jesus,
and the Day of Judgment
which was coming soon.
He wouldn't leave us alone.
Not even a downpour enough
to deter him. I kept busy
with my camera while he
invoked the four horsemen
to a mystified Japanese girl.

Hard to find the motel
Rosemary recommended.
We had to double back
to the last exit, where streamers
fluttered over gas pumps.
Turning from the highway
toward the horizon – the sky
was perfectly clear now, golden
with sunset – there seemed nothing else
but the wind and rolling Coke cans
between me and the North Pole.

Rand McNally

The route, if it wasn't through mountains
in northern lands broken by glaciers, kept
to the contours, crossing plaited water-courses
split by sandbanks and bushy islands.

Furrow-puddles glinted and swirled
as we hit the boggy bottom land of Arkansas.
Dappled horses turned toward the car
from a blue pond in a broad meadow.

Flickering underleaves of tamarisk,
cottonwood, wild olive and willow
carried the Rio Grande past Albuquerque.
Pine reflections snagged in Taos gorge.

The current of the Little Colorado
was terracotta like dissolving pottery.
The Missouri near Omaha and the Mississippi
at Rock Island bracketed Iowa.

I saw the tarred beaches of Lake Erie,
muddy Susquehannah's meandering valley.
Woods now instead of forests,
the planet growing its green fur.

Not compass circles, but stains from coffee cups.
My Rand McNally Atlas falls loose from its staples.

Between the Canyons: the Navajo Sibyl

On the rim of the canyon, between
the canyons, rifts and gashes
in the earth's carcass (tarry scabs
of broken badlands, clotted red
of its inner body), a storm woke you
at three a.m. in the motel near
the clinic for alcoholics. Full moon
thunder flash and lightning strobe.

Sluggish green and seeming-harmless
at the lowest level sliced through aeons
the river had pulverised boulders
polished the cliff face blocking caves
where buried gods spit out
Time's soporific layer-cake
and shrug their painted shoulders. Earthy
patterns ripple as they move closer.

Magnetic, cosmic, geological,
the energy was actual,
demanded absolute homage.
You were its chosen medium
and focus: a substance tested
to the limit of endurance, flattened
against the planet's raw surface
like a fly on a windscreen.

Survival of the Cult

Osiris's head is buried like seed-corn
at Abydos. His temple is built west
of the river, near the edge of the desert.
He was called 'Chief of the Westerners'.

Over his recumbent body
on the sanctuary frieze, Isis hovers.
Wing over wing, through fanning sun rays
above the palm trees, two kites glide.

The covered well and stone seats
at the side of the road are plastered
blue, red striped. Old men lounge there –
watch the youngsters fight, the laughing

gangs of headscarved girls in gaudy
garments – argue, spit and boast,
while black-swathed pregnant women pour
water into plastic pails.

'The Mother of Pots' – grey mounds
of shattered votive jars that pilgrims
brought in pharaohs' times – stretches
between the temple and the village.

Some houses are decorated
with holy words and drawings of boats, planes
and the black rock of the Kaaba. A man
who lives there made the journey to Mecca.

On every painted wall, holding
his crook and flail – still the protector –
corn-crowned and mummy-linen robed,
Lord Osiris is part of the picture.

Bouzigues

There's a place on the road
coming down from the hills where rows
of oyster frames unfurl
on an indigo sea
like a pattern of bamboo fans
or blocks of pale embroidery
on a geisha's kimono,
whose knees and shoulders
press against the border
of the wood engraving
tight as Alice's
when she started growing.

The high-piled mass
of the dead volcano cone
is her oiled and twisted hair
fighting free from its combs
to tangle in the shell–
encrusted poles. Her eyes
look crazed. A small tooth shows
between pursed lips, and one breast's
tip in the oyster scent
of watered silk's
loosened folds. Her mood is
storm clouds over the lagoon.

Blossom and Technology

I wasn't sure what to expect,
after flying for eighteen hours
over the Pole. Japan
was contradictory images:
stone and technology,
crowds and cherry blossom.

I came too late for the blossom,
the one sight I did expect,
as if technology
could slow seasons and hours
till certain images
confirmed: this is Japan.

Some things were strange in Japan:
not the imitation blossom,
but those plastic images
of meals you might expect
in restaurants. The hours
to make them, the technology!

An older technology
had created another Japan
where no count was taken of hours
spent training flowers to blossom
in a place you wouldn't expect,
or painting a screen with their images.

I wanted to keep those images.
My camera – technology
of the sort I came to expect
from anything bought in Japan –

was aimed at every blossom
and stone as it changed with the hours.

I stood and watched for hours
near the temple images
people's faces blossom:
prayer's technology
must be what fuels Japan,
which is not what you'd expect,

nor expect that so few hours
in Japan could reconcile images
of blossom and technology.

The Japanese Bath

I feared my heart would stop: the depth and heat
of water in the wooden tub, the thought
that even if I called you would not hear
from where you sat, beyond the ante-room,
silk-kimono'd by the painted screen.
I stretched my legs out, saw my body small
as a court lady of Kyoto, green
as moss around a temple garden pool
carp-filled, and how the same droplets of steam
frosting my hair beaded the darkened walls.
The silent isolation made me feel:
to come this far and drown could be foredoomed.
Then I stood up, showered off the dream
and ghosts with cold water, calm now, and cleaned.

Japanese Syllabics

When the tea-master's disciples praised
Kobori Enshu's beautiful scrolls
and plates, saying that no one could help
but admire them, he sorrowfully
answered: 'This only proves how common-
place I am.' His dissatisfaction
at their response quite opposite to
my constant need for reassurance,
my placatory smile – the nodding
head-piece of a jointed wooden doll,
agreeing, agreeing.

                Legend tells
how he built the Katsura villa
on the following conditions: no
limits on money or manpower
or time, and no one to disturb his
conception of temples and gardens
and pavilions by seeing the work
until finished. He was so secure
in his judgement, knew what he wanted.

Each gesture and implement exact,
the simple tea-ceremony is
a junction of choices, decisions;
its purpose (or am I imposing
an alien system of values
and totally misunderstanding?)
to enact and confirm a balance
calmness and grace I yearn for and lack.

Yet even such a grand tea-master
could doubt his purity of motive,
lament a lack of courage, wonder
whether his most precious treasure had
been chosen more to please others than
because it was to his own taste.

                    Now
I'll show you my favourite puppet:
black brows, white face, and fluttering sleeves.
Her expression is so fine-drawn that
the painted features seem to change with
my opinions. But when she's being
praised, or when I'm confident enough
to stop equivocating, then how
balanced, calm and graceful we become.

Incense

A dull shine like black ice:
the bronze urn at the top of the stone
steps, its incised pattern the same pale
colour as the ash that fills it – from how
many millions of burned-out incense sticks?

Shiomi told me I could light one
if I wished. I watched the other mourners
pass their hands through the swirling smoke,
smooth it over their heads and waft
it down the fronts of their kimonos.

The red tips of the incense sticks
pulsed and glowed in the shadow of cedar
pillars and temple roof tiles as I
bent close, murmuring prayers and names,
half a world from where they lay,

yet certain they were here with me,
supportive spirits among this strangeness.
The shrine doors swing shut in the wind
and the incense billows. Three women
laugh as though it means good luck.

Keeper

Mother's fur coats,
silver teapot and velvet
boxes of broken ear-rings.

Aunt Ann's crackle-glass lamp
with its patterned parchment shade,
her mahogany bookcase.

Daddy's volumes of Jewish Thoughts,
A Hermit in the Himalayas,
those plaid plus-fours.

A faded suitcase, corded,
the sort a schoolboy uses,
full of Harry's notebooks.

Albums of glossy photos.
The last smile dimmed,
since I heard about cousin Fanny.

I see the family face
break through the surface
of Grandpa's speckled mirror

and hardly recognise myself.
Every object
claims me as its keeper,

souvenirs of joy
and anger I'm not sure whether
I want to cherish or destroy.

Learning About Him

A sheep bleated, and sounded
exactly like someone imitating a sheep,
which made me think of my father –

the sort of thing he'd do,
suddenly start to clown and act crazy, or like
a warning cough of static

from the jelly-mould
Art Deco shape of the big valve radio,
its glowing amber dial

marked with places he'd been to.
I'd twiddle the knobs and move the needle through
London, Bombay, Rio.

'Look after my Feigele,'
(the Yiddish name meant little bird) her dying
mother said to the lodger,

my father, so they got married.
I heard the story after his funeral
and finally understood

why I was born in New York.
I'd recognised another melancholic,
but not the autodidact's

hunger (we shared that too)
he dissembled – as though it would be shameful
if any of us knew –

for self-improvement, until
clearing his room, choosing which books to keep,
I found old favourites.

I hate to read books marked
with comments in the margin, underlinings,
but these were different.

I was learning about him.
For instance, how he'd saved what seemed every
postcard I'd mailed home –

grudgingly dutiful –
and pasted them in scrapbooks, marking my routes
red and his bright blue.

We'd almost meshed the globe.
I wonder if his restlessness was soothed
by mine, or irritated?

Dear father, now your crazy
daughter's weeping sounds like bleating or
a faulty radio.

'Softly Awakes My Heart . . .'

Saint-Saëns aria
chosen by a man in Saudi Arabia
for his daughter in Ghana:
a Sunday morning World Service broadcast.
(That version on His Master's Voice.)

It brings a complex recall
of dusty velvet armchairs
a pile of records and the old victrola
net curtains faded and crisp
from sunlight through the dining room French window.

The mezzo-soprano
would smooth your mouth and eyes.
Your whole body calm except for
one hand turning on its wrist, accompanying.
I preferred a harsher music then.

Towards My Waiting Mother

The animal decency of my father's death.
With vacant bright gaze that could not be
deflected understood or met, like a forest
creature who crawls into a hollow tree
or ditch when its time has come, he curved around
the smallest possible space in the hospital bed.

He didn't talk much – none of the stories
I'd hoped at last to hear, which only now
I realise that I expected (still
the child demanding his attention). Instead,
how simple everything seemed as he moved further
away from me, towards my waiting mother.

Those Photographs

Always the rowdy one, pushing
toward the centre, the one demanding
absolute attention, who had to be
Daddy's little darling:
the beam in my eye still only lets me
notice how hard the others are trying.

Those photographs. I'm sure we sent him
hundreds, during the war. The reason
I'm standing that close to my mother
near the porch steps, like a sapling
not yet grown free of its root-stock,
is to lean against her and keep my balance.

Don't laugh at that dress: gauzy white cotton,
green-checked, was my version of a dryad's
costume. Barefoot, on tiptoe, I'm squinting
because I took my glasses off
and held them awkwardly behind
my back, to look older and glamorous.

She looks what she'd been born as:
a shrewd, ironic Jewish peasant
who knew competing daughters are best
ignored. Her indifference drove me quite
berserk. For years I fought it. But she slept
at concerts, and in museums her shoes hurt.

Her body was so medieval.
Big head, short legs and narrow shoulders,
a pelvis and belly to carry dozens,
the small teeth and strong jaw of an ogre.

There was no grace to her feet or hands.
I think she is my feminine ideal,

as every blue-eyed hero
became my father's opposite
in honour of that taboo.
She made me a shape-shifter, whatever
it seemed was wanted: all things
to all men. Except hers.

Station Road

Fond memories of the garden shed
behind our ground floor flat in Station Road.

Daddy talked about the Oxford Group
and Chamberlain. Grandpa said:
'Be good, sweet maid, and let who will be clever.'
I thought up riddles to confound him
and shouted all the facts I'd read.

Mother pushed me into bed with shoes on
and tied a rag around my neck
when the school inspector called. 'She has a fever.'
I've forgotten why she kept me home
but not my admiration for her lawless style.

Privacy in the high-ceilinged toilet:
pressing fists against my eyes I saw
kaleidoscopes and arabesques.

After ballet class, walking to the shop
which sold black liquorice straps
and envelopes of Japanese paper flowers
that unfolded and blossomed in a glass of water,
we sang: 'Under the spreading chestnut tree,
it's time to join the ARP.'

My brother slept in a deep square pram
under a tree in the front garden.
I stopped to peer beneath the hood.
The blank, glistening white ellipses
of his eyes rolled back

behind half-shut, delicate, violet-webbed lids
were another sign the war was coming closer.

That was when I wanted to be Tarzan,
teased and nagged till Mother bought
two lengths of cloth so I could cut brown spots
and stitch them to the pale, to make a leopard skin.

My friends from the house around the corner
could only wear one-colour costumes
and had to obey, whatever I ordered.

I can remember how I lured
my willing victims between the spiderwebs
upended broken chairs and rusting
earth-caked forks and spades, how,
among the dustmotes of teatime sunlight
and moulting plumes of last year's pampas grass
that made us sneeze, we tried out faulty versions
of being grown-up – as if the future
wouldn't offer time enough.

My Fuchsia

My fuchsia is a middle-aged woman
who's had fourteen children, and though
she could do it again, she's rather tired.

All through the summer, new blooms.
I'm amazed. But the purple and crimson
have paled. Some leaves are yellowed or withering.

These buds look weaker and smaller,
like menopause babies. Yet still
she's a gallant fine creature performing her function.

– That's how they talk about women,
and I heard myself using the same sort of language.
Then I understood my love for August:
its exhausted fertility
after glut and harvest.

Out in the garden, playing
at being a peasant forced
to slave until dark with a child on my back

another at the breast and probably
pregnant, I remember
wondering if I'd ever manage

the rites of passage from girl
to woman: fear
and fascination hard to choose between.

Thirty years later, I pick the crumpled flowers
off the fuchsia plant and water it
as if before the shrine
of two unknown grandmothers –
and my mother, who was a fourteenth child.

The Crescent

My stick of lipsalve is worn away
into the same curved crescent
that was the first thing I noticed
about my mother's lipstick.
It marked the pressure of her existence
upon the world of matter.

Imagine the grim fixity
of my stare, watching her smear
the vivid grease across her lips
from a tube shiny as a bullet.
The way she smoothed it
with the tip of a little finger
(the tinge it left, even after
washing her hands, explained
the name 'pinky') and her pointed tongue
licking out like a kitten's,
fascinated, irritated.

It was part of the mystery of
brassières and compacts and handbags
that meant being grown-up. I thought
my own heels would have to grow
a sort of spur to squeeze right down
the narrow hollow inside high heels.

Now I am calmer and no longer
paint my lips except with this,
pale as a koshered carcass
drained of blood in salty water
or a memorial candle,
wax congealed down one side,

as though it stood in the wind
that blows from the past, flame
reflected like a crescent
moon against a cloud
in the pool of molten light.

I carry the sign of the moon
and my mother, a talisman
in a small plastic tube
in my handbag, a holy relic
melted by believers'
kisses, and every time
I smooth my lips with the unguent
I feel them pout and widen
in the eternal smile
of her survival through me,
feel her mouth on mine.

The Fabric

My mother's glee, ripping half-rotten cloth
fibres weakened by countless washings
towels twisted and wrung out too often
unravelling cuffs and collars
laddered stockings
pyjamas split at the crotch.
How can I forget her expression.
Her hands are white with tension.

After thirty or forty years
mending the linen caring for things
what a release what freedom
to wrench the weave tear the weft and warp
into smaller and smaller pieces
until totally useless.
Something always goes wrong enough
not to be mended except by death.

The snap as each strand parts
is harsh as the rattle of gunfire
but the strips are too narrow for bandages.
Fragments of lint swirl in the air
dustmotes in sunlight swarming locusts
drift of duckweed on the water's surface.
Her laughter is a thread in the fabric
that nets the furthest stars.

A Discussion with Patrick Kavanagh

(about his poem 'Intimate Parnassus')

I could sit here for hours, twisting my rings,
dazed by the light and colour a diamond flashes,
without a thought in my head. An image which must
include everything that went to form me:
the universal gases, ultraviolet
infra-red, the seams of giant ferns
compressed to carbon. My mother's photo album.

'. . . to be/ Passive, observing with a steady eye,'
is the poet's purpose, you wrote, praising
a god-like detachment (another world entirely,
but who would want to argue?) Trying to calm
my frantic heart with such-like axioms
I would guess is not exactly what
you meant, but still the only path I know

apart from total recall: the paraphernalia
of personality – too much baggage
there for transmutation. Staring
in the crystal ball of my mother's diamond ring
doesn't serve to clarify connections
fused by violent words and acts. The conflict
between poetry and contemplation.

To be passive, observing with a steady eye
(the only duty I acknowledge) needs
a cool ironic style I've not yet managed.
And pondering one's destiny is suspect
from whatever viewpoint, even Parnassus;
forces the language to defensive postures.
My mother's ringless hands keep turning the pages.

The Propeller

The hazard sign on your door
like a spinning propeller – meaning
radiation. You seemed to cringe
at the top of the bed, so pale,
and I cringed back to the room's corner.

Invisible, the cobalt rods
in the breast you showed me (it was dark
as liver, like the breast of a woman
kicked to death in a pogrom)
but I imagined them

swords through the breast of a blue madonna,
rays from the guns of space monsters,
treasure spilled from a wreck
on the spines of a coral reef
glinting under the water.

I wanted to behave
in a civilised way, like a grown-up,
but couldn't make myself get nearer.
I noted your rueful smile.
You'd already lived that fear.

The licence plates on my taxi
had those three magic letters
for my name, Mother's, Father's.
But I knew they wouldn't save me
from your scything propeller.

Mothers in Shakespeare

Jenny in bed, watching her mother at the typewriter
snatching another line of *Hamlet* between dictated
sentences, while Father paces back and forth.
The longer the pauses, the gladder Jenny's mother is.
Otherwise, she loses the flow of the dialogue.

Jenny grown-up, phoning around, talking of mothers
and fathers, and how Shakespeare must have worked. 'Just like
my mother – taking it down in shorthand. "Come on, chaps,"
he said. "Let's get something together for Twelfth Night".
All of them were men, I want you to understand.'

Jenny remembering her mother's death. Being
'the writer's wife' wasn't enough: she drew her last breath
over an unlit gas-poker. 'Will had his actors to play with.
What did my mother have?' she wails down the mouthpiece, falls
back on the pillow and stares at the ceiling, alone in the
house.

Jenny wants a poem about her mother and Shakespeare,
love and violent death. 'Now the kids have left home –
just like their father did – I think how few they are,
mothers in Shakespeare. Hermione was a dupe. Lady
Macbeth was right. And none would ever have done his
typing.'

Like Manet's 'Olympe'

Like Manet's 'Olympe', naked in the afternoon heat
and manilla-shaded light, my aunt lay
on the green watered-silk of her bedspread. Smooth hair,
proud head, short but shapely legs and
high breasts were so much the same as the painting
I had just fallen in love with, that I faltered, still
half in the doorway, almost afraid to enter.

Through one moted beam that cut across the room
between us, I saw her reflection, pale as an ocean
creature, floating deep in the dressing-table mirror
over splinters of sun from the jumble of bottles
and jars – stern eyes seeming to dare me closer.

But this was a small house in Virginia, not
the Paris of artists. In spite of leather-bound volumes
of Schopenhauer and Baudelaire and Saturday
opera broadcasts, her aesthetic was helpless
against suburban power. The loneliness
and vanity and fearfulness which kept her
from dalliance made me the only possible
audience, and her adoring victim.

About art and beauty, loneliness and
fearfulness and vanity, how much she taught me.

Ovid Among the Scythians

(Delacroix)

Marshy banks of the Danube, reeds and bushes
and muddy crescents of horses' hooves. Their
clothes are earth-coloured, his dark blue.

He feels the autumn starting – that sky, those clouds,
the way the wind is moving them. The mountains
roll back, uncharted as far as China.

Ovid is writing another letter to Rome –
a gentle puzzlement to his watchers, which weapons
and dogs don't quite shield them from.

He wonders whether a linen toga, his scrolls
and pens, and their unknowing admiration,
can be protection against such sadness,

if he can metamorphose Chaos to Order,
exile to Fate, the amorous summer weasel
into the noble winter ermine.

Unique Forms

Umberto Boccioni, what you did
with metal: this striding concept,
a Proteus of the four dimensions
to celebrate the sequent moment,
objectify dynamic movement –
I want to do with words.

Is it streaming from the past or future,
the force that deforms and defines
this science fiction Crusader battling forward
through its turbulence? (Fluttering banners,
spurs, trapping and helmet, a cross borne aloft.
Then trenches, searchlights, bombs.)

I note the dates. Pure sensation
speed and violence now
are standard fashion, that fierce manifesto
just another historical relic.
But your shape-shifter still maintains unique
forms of continuity in time and space.

Umberto Boccioni, 1882–1916
Marinetti's Futurist Manifesto, 1909
'Unique Forms of Continuity in Space', 1913

Driving I

Umber, amber, ochre. Viridian and sepia.
A Victorian painting: 'After the Storm'.
The branches seem wrenched by a torturing bully.
Tested and found wanting – a character corroded
by putting money on the wrong horse.
Faster, faster.
The purpose of writing notes
is that the words are not spoken: a system
that would be shattered by articulation.
Sounds heard with the inner ear
surface as slowly
as other disturbances you learn to ignore.
Clay-smeared discs of sawn tree-trunks
like split stones or stained amoebas
annular pools in the fields like the roots of clouds.
The one who gets blamed always has the power.
Driving is the metaphor.

Driving II

Each species is allotted its number of heartbeats.
A mouse has the same life span as myself or a whale
but lives it more quickly, at a different tempo.

The fluttering heat of a heart or a forest.
How many leaves to a kilometre?
I want to be astonished, but it happens less often.

Such solid coils of steam and smoke extruded from
the tall cone-chimneys of a power station,
like chalky turds defying the laws of gravity.

Trees and cars and clouds blur in the speed. I have seen
almost enough for a whole life – endless renewal
and repetition. The planet belongs to the trees.

Driving III

Village after village, evidence
filters from the back of the café
louder than the lotto numbers –
people laughing, dogs barking.

A frieze of bright brown chickens
with scarlet combs
who strut and scratch below the hedge,
running interference.

Iron body oozing rust
into the wooden cross,
roadside crucifixes
transubstantiate to brioche.

Behind the garage, a car jacked up
at the inspection pit
like a woman with her legs
in obstetrical stirrups.

The museums of Europe
are textbooks for martyrs.
The river barges inspire noyades.
Two people dragging each other down.

The Dead Sea

Nights I don't sleep, however I lie
every limb and organ aches
and though I stretch further up
the pillows, throw the blanket back,
I still can't breathe and the dark vibrates

its molecules into a form
pressing me close from mouth to hip,
stifled under an embrace more
urgent than any human lover's,
when I become his favourite

to float with him upon a sea
of melted bones and curdled clouds
and phosphorescent glass towards
a hidden shore we never reach
through waters where we cannot drown.

The Planetarium

It makes a difference
whether the earth is at its winter
nearness to, or summer
distance from, the sun.

A few hundred miles change climate
and terrain from ice
to jungle, north to south,
every fact of life.

Which seems strange, compared
to the vastnesses of space
(my first visit
to the Planetarium

fixed an image of blackness
struggling against
a fragile net of light)
yet comforting, because

a millimetre's alteration
in the angle at
the corner of your mouth
can have the same importance.

Rosebay Willow-herb

Rosebay willow-herb in clumps
among the brambles,
as bushy as my hair was then.

I wrote those words
yesterday, then spent the evening
and all today
in search of a connection between
rosebay and hair,
went thirty years back, trying to bring
it through to the present.

We'd walked across the stubbled fields
looking for somewhere
to lie, while a combine harvester
working nearby
returned and retreated, louder and softer.
Off the path
a bale of straw's dusty chaff
served well enough.

Our parched hands and mouths, deprived
too long of what
they wanted, a touch as irritating
and electric
as rosebay down on skin and cloth,
urgently clung.

Our starved eyes craved colours
in close-up – fleshy
pinks and purples like the willow-herb
flowers that clustered

at the ditch's hidden edge
and challenged the sunset.

When we stood up, my hair was full
of fluffy down
and straw. I had to comb it out
before we parted.

I remember the stripped pallor
of flat fields
under a glowing sky, the shadow
of dark-leaved trees
along the hedge, as if a small
enamelled picture,
an amulet to guard me till
our next meeting,

and I know why, every August
since, my hair
feels tangled with rosebay willow-herb.

String

Unknotting the string you tied
my fingers make the same movements
but in the opposite order
undoing what you did

while smoothness sheathes my skin
with its electric aura
as if our hands entangled
space and time

and the rough twine recalls
your morning face,
tales of knots impossible
to loose – how they were untied.

Cartography

                    In every room you've had
I've lain back on the bed
                    or in a chair and while
you've fondled and caressed me
                    over your shoulder
eyes narrowing with pleasure
                    before they open wide
I've stared at shapes and patterns
                    symbols for swamp and heathland
highways' venous systems
                    concentric irregular
contour lines that tilt
                    lake to valley to mountain
aniline intensities
                    of mineral strata
deepening oceanic tints
                    the Irriwaddy Delta
Spitzbergen   Deception Island
                    imagining the planet's
surface folds and hollows
                    swelling smoothness
the secrets of its massive body.
                    Who's been the navigator
who the cartographer?

High Pressure Zone

Smoke from the bonfires and fireworks of Guy Fawkes night
combined with a high pressure zone and a clear calm sky
doesn't seem to add up to much, and yet was enough
to cover the whole country next morning with fog.

Your changes of mood, or mine, consume days
as the foulness bounces back and forth like claps of thunder
between curdling clouds. You say: 'You get rid of your hurt
by passing it on to me.' I think you do the same.

It's something like: 'For want of a nail the battle was lost'.
Every thing affects everything else, and the truisms
become truer. We walked to the square to watch the fires.
When I saw the children waving sparklers to make patterns
against the dark, I knew that we were in the last part
of our lives. But if nothing ends, how can we two die?

'Don't Wake Me'

My 'Don't wake me' notes. Yawning
at the kitchen table under
the oily glare of a lightbulb that smears
out shadows from each fallen crumb
and gouges cracks in the ceiling.
But disorder doesn't signify –
I've never seen the place before.

Strange. For when I lay in bed
not able to sleep or get up either,
only the thought that the plumber was due
quite soon really, and I should write
a note to tell you, finally stirred me.
I could ruminate the bitter cud
for hours, in an anxious stupor.

'Don't wake me,' they usually open.
'It's 3.45am and Lopez
said he'd come at 8.30.'
'Don't wake me, please. It's 4.52.
But don't forget –' something or other.
I rely on you absolutely.
I put it all on your shoulders.

A more exalted purpose
rarely forces pen to paper such dawn
moments. Last night I slept, but dreamed of
bursting cisterns and insolent servants –
a world in turmoil. If you'd snored
or moaned and woken me, that note
might have become a poem.

Sister, Sister

Sister, sister, I am sick.
Come and give me meat and drink.
Let me eat from your hand.

     *   *   *

Amnon lay on his bed, moaning
with lust and vexation, knowing
that Tamar was still a virgin

by the special colour of her dress.
(Such was the custom for a princess.)
'Come closer, sister, you

yourself shall be my meat and drink.'
He ran his tongue around her wrist.
She could not make him stop.

'The sweetest food is your hair and flesh.'
First he wheedled, then he threatened.
She argued, 'Do not force me.'

Those words meant less to him than the insects'
drone outside the curtained window
or incense fumes trapped

between the roofbeams, and he was stronger.
Afterwards, he could no longer
bear that tragic face,

called a servant to bolt the door
and keep the woman out. She tore
the bodice of her dress

(lost, the right to wear it now)
daubed with ashes head and brow,
hurt more by his hatred

than her ravishment. What
did Tamar think when Absalom,
two years later, killed him?

The story leaves her desolate,
but doesn't tell. One has to guess.
I imagine Tamar

in her chamber, burning incense
and remembering. The insects'
whining seems a song:

'Sister, sister, I am sick.
Come and give me meat and drink.
Let me eat from your hand.'

Cup and Sword

The cup has to be stone,
cup-holes
in the lower face of the protecting boulder
dripping stone-milk.

Which means that the sword
is Excalibur –
King Arthur's slashing sword –
hard-belly, the voracious one.

Those bodies in bloody armour
were knights-errant
who fought to hold their cavern,
keep the cup hidden.

Something that started a long time ago
can still nourish –
like a Grail story –
though the cup is empty, the sword broken.

Evil Enters

Evil enters when there is no answer
so don't ask any questions.
You want to know too much.

For instance, are those half-seen figures
moving up and down a ladder
angels, demons, snakes,
or other souls in the same dull torment?
The Sphinx and Oedipus?
You'd wrestle hard, and all night through,
just for the company and some response.

Before dawn broke, surely
there'd be a gasp or groan you could interpret
as a revelation,
a whole theology – and you its prophet –
whatever best diverts your rage and grief.

Evil enters when there is no answer,
so don't ask any questions.
But you can't make yourself stop.

A Room

That room is too dark for me.
There are things in that room I don't want to see.
That door has been closed for a long time.

The most I can do at first
is change the wooden panels for glass.
The black ovals of my spectacles
flash blue when my head is raised, and white
shapes of clouds move across them.

Light dissolves the doorframe
to a glowing margin, but the paths
I've walked in every mood and season
show clear as through the rifling
of a telescope: memory's target.

Trees form the walls of a green room.
Between the restless branches, sunlight
glazes rose-windows.

The Restlessness of Sunset

I pull the curtains to
open them again
get up from my desk
sit down stand up again

to go to the window
and watch the changes
of cloud and colour
every moment changing

and every afternoon
as dusk begins
I can't stay still
or close myself in

until the sun has gone
behind the trees below the line
of the horizon
until the sky

has dulled and darkened
enough to let
the evening start
and soothe the restlessness of sunset.

The Limitations of Tiredness

The fierce hiss of sap in a burning log
is the same sound sleep makes as it withdraws
from me when I lie down for a nap these winter
afternoons. At first my hands relax and
warmth spreads through limbs which suddenly seem
larger. The blue and brown of moving skies
and surging water as the tide pulls out
across the sand-flats concentrate between
my brows, above my nose, into a point
of light I stare at while the noise gets louder.
I never know why it stops, why, with a heart-
lurch and a deep-drawn breath of alarm I turn
back to the room and fire and desk and wake
to a stormy dusk, the limitations of tiredness.

The Same Power

Lush chill of spring in Holland Park.
Dark glassy flesh of the bluebells, hoarse
cry of a peacock strutting his courtship cope
against a wind which flattens it out behind
and ripples the quills like waves on a squally sea.
Striated bark of birch trees' pale trunks
as sharp a white as opening hawthorn flowers.
Vivid rainclouds scudding across the sky.

Which all must be attended to now,
not half-ignored, then recalled later –
that common regret for not having been alert
enough to recognise the one moment
when beauty, truth, life and death became
the same Power: evoked not described.

The Poet –

      sits at her desk, watching an insect
moving its antennae in time
with Mozart. A quiet evening in August,

invoking the melancholy pleasure
of aimless thought. Knowing that what
goes unrecorded is written on water.
The ripples disperse, as is their nature.

But beyond the roofs, the crescent
moon and stars seem points and markers
of a limitless expansion.

Later, she might wonder whether
something precious was squandered, ointments
poured extravagantly out
(almost swooning from the odours).

The torment starts whose cure is nothing less
than pen and ink and paper –
      and the entire universe.

That Presence

Like a painter stepping backward from the easel,
straightening up from the worktable,
with a loaded brush, to see exactly where
another touch of red is wanted, like
a carpet weaver wondering if the time
has come to change the pattern, a sculptor
hesitating before the first decisive cut,
I ponder a poem, repeating every word,
trying to hear where a note needs altering,
testing by breath and sense and luck,

like staring at the surface of a mirror
through soundless levels between glass and silver
into the pupils of that reflected presence
over my shoulder advancing from its depths.

Autumn Garden Poem

I want to know the name of those leaves,
pale and felted one side
smooth and green

the other, like strips of paper torn
from an endless scroll and strewn
across the lawn.

        * * *

Two Japanese ladies, leaning
fondly as lovers: a willow's
ragged sleeves

brushing the grass. The jade-blue discs
silvered by dew and frost
from a eucalyptus

bush are their broken necklaces.
Spiders' webs have tangled
their plaited tresses.

        * * *

I can show you rosebay and golden
rod, moulting thistles
and rusty clover.

But what are those pallid flowers called
that open in sunlight, and close
when the evening falls?

The Wittersham Sibyl

The pattern of dew on spiders' webs
and how it hung like crystal beads,
every hole the birds had torn –
pucker-edged and starfish-shaped
for frost and rain to work upon –
through fallen apples lacquer-bright
among the swathes of dripping fern,

these, and the angles the rising wind
bent from the pampas' papery leaves
and straw-pale peeling stems, the way
the shattered-topaz acorn husks
livid toadstools and rusty moss
reclaimed the lawn, she knew must be
messages from the god.

The Same Ease

Walking in the square, through the damp and misty, still mild
    air of a late October Sunday morning.
Only at the second circuit do I meet another person: a young
    family, parents and children,
but otherwise the paths are empty – and the tennis court, the
    sandpit and climbing frame, seventeen acres
(do I remember the size correctly?) of grass and flowers, shrubs
    and trees: the delicious colours of the leaves
and their softened texture like the gloves and handbag from the
    wardrobe of an ageing elegant woman;
the last few roses, gnarled buds scentless this late in the year;
    some stalky toadstools: as if all for my sole pleasure.
Suddenly I think it's raining – not that I feel the drops, but
    because of the sound – and watch a shower
of leaves detach from their branch with the same ease, the momen
    come to let go, that I hope for.

The Novelty

Winter's charcoal structures and autumn's flaring challenge
after summer fattens spring's sketchy foliage:
like a million gas-jets,
crocuses ignite beneath the warming boughs.

Meadows flushing green for what seems just a day
before their tawny paleness is stacked away as harvest,
ponds sink low and hedges wither.
Lambs becoming sheep, and babies, parents.

Then months of frost and clouded skies until the change
from open fires to windows; and as the sun approaches
the extreme of solstice,
the novelty of watching it all start again.

Residence Secondaire

Christmas Day (which was sunny and calm, with not one
cloud in the sky) we planted thirty-five fir trees
to grow a wall between ours and the next garden.
It was a shock to see that large pink house loom up
so gaunt and high, after summer's green enclosure,
once the chestnut and acacia leaves had fallen.

Some have blue-tinged foliage, others look golden.
We didn't notice, or choose them especially,
but it seems a happy omen. Variation
is promised, a flicker between the primary
colours that combine to make green, like the vivid
brushstrokes in the dense impasto of a painting.

Today, the fourth of January, the weather
still fine, we bought three-metre bamboo stakes, cut them
in half and hammered them into the earth, to hold
the trees firm against the north wind – Tramontana
it's called here – help them survive the hardest part of
winter. They'll be alive next time we come, I hope.

The garden was abandoned for decades. Under
the brambles we discovered a half-dead box hedge,
stone-bordered flowerbeds, roses and fruit trees gone back
to the wild. Ivy smothered the lilacs and lapped
the steps, twisted around the wire-mesh fence, and wove
a net that had to be unravelled strand by strand.

Planting and clearing, not wanting to change things much,
we are taking possession – and being possessed.
What could be more demanding than a garden? 'Don't
start work on the garden!' friends warned, 'or you'll never
get away.' But we bought the house because of
the garden. We are putting down roots in the garden.

In Drummond's Room

(William Drummond of Hawthornden, 1585–1649)

This morning, after
lighting the fire, I looked
from the deep window of Drummond's room

over the glen
toward clouds so dark that the black
horizon-trees blurred against them.

Only the flames were bright,
burning under the pilgrims'
scallop-shells carved on the mantel.

Then the wind veered,
the wood smoked, and the tall yew
whose needled boughs

fill the other window
soughed, louder than
the logs' seething, and through the glass

splinters of colour –
the red excited push
of growth, the yellow of last year's leaves

that strengthens green,
patches of blue, sun and shadow –
signalled a new front

of weather moving in.
For an hour or two at noon
the sky was clear. But I prefer

to stay in here
and build the fire up, squeeze
the bellows, watch exactly how

sparks jump and
the cinders shimmer, how
the branches turn and lift at the same

agitated angle
as the sudden-falling slant
of whirling snow that will not settle

and the calm curve
of the sunset rainbow
above the swollen river,

to disentangle
the single pattern through each
recurrence and renewal since

he stared into the fire
and from the windows, to see
and feel and think what I do now.

Notes

The Neville Brothers
A New Orleans rhythm and blues group.

Krishna grew up among a group of milkmaids who were entranced by the sound of his flute. He was the eighth incarnation of Vishnu, and is worshipped in the form of the Juggernaut at the temple at Puri on the Bay of Bengal.

Rock Island
A hamlet in mid Tennessee, USA; not the city of the same name referred to in *Rand McNally*.

In Tuscaloosa
A town in Alabama, USA.

Survival of the Cult
Abydos, a town on the west bank of the Nile, about 300 miles south of Cairo, was seat of the worship of Osiris in ancient Egypt. Egyptians from all walks of life aspired to be buried there.

The Western Land was the land of the dead. Osiris was Lord of the Dead, and Chief of the Westerners.

Osiris's sister, Isis, collected the scattered parts of his body after their brother Seth had murdered him, and buried them at Abydos.

The black rock of the Kaaba is the sacred shrine of Islam in the middle of the great mosque at Mecca.

Bouzigues
A village on the Bassin de Thau, on the south coast of France, famous for its oysters. The lagoon is closed at each end by the extinct volcanic cones of Sete and Agde.

Japanese Syllabics
Kobori Enshu (1576–1647) built the Katsura Rikyu in Kyoto for Toyotomi Hideyoshi, exacting the three famous conditions, and helped the tea-ceremony survive this period of Japanese history.

Station Road
ARP – the Air Raid Precautions. A civilian organization for protection against air raids, formed in England at the start of the Second World War.